DEEP WISDOM,
HOLY STRUGGLE

Exploring the Radical Christian Life

By Barbara Cawthorne Crafton

Introduction by Joan Chittister

Forward Movement
Cincinnati, Ohio

Trinity Wall Street
New York, New York

Forward
Movement

Trinity
WALL STREET

DEEP WISDOM,
HOLY STRUGGLE

Exploring the Radical Christian Life

By Barbara Cawthorne Crafton

Introduction by Joan Chittister

Table of Contents

Preface

The Benedictine life is one of contemplation birthing action. It is at once profoundly spiritual and immensely practical: it expects its principles to bear fruit that transforms both the people within the community and the world outside. In no sense is it otherworldly—even though Benedictines observe the hours of prayer and silent meditation, they expect the love and work of their active lives to flow from that contemplation. They do not believe that there are two kinds of people, the active and the contemplative. They believe we are all both of these.

This book focuses on Joan Chittister's introduction to her year of daily meditations entitled *The Radical Christian Life*. Her introduction, which is reprinted in this guide, serves as valuable preparation for anyone using *The Radical Christian Life* as an aid to a closer walk with Christ. *The Radical Christian Life* takes twelve of the many stories about St. Benedict—one for each month of the year—and approaches them in unexpected ways.

Often, we read these stories the same way we might read stories about Paul Bunyan or some other legendary character: tall tales about someone much larger than life.

But Joan Chittister doesn't do that: these stories, even the fantastic ones—like the one in which Benedict enables a young monk to run on water—serve to draw us back into the enormous possibilities of our most ordinary daily struggles. Similarly, Chittister's introduction recasts for us an institutional history well known to a Benedictine audience, placing it in a wider application and making it accessible for use by anyone.

— Barbara Cawthorne Crafton

How to Use this Book

The stories and Chittister's musings on them will furnish ample material for meditation each day. You might use the meditations in *The Radical Christian Life* as a support to your daily prayer, a little something to read each day to quicken your spirit's interest. You might meet with others on a regular basis to respond together to what you read day by day as individuals.

The introduction from *The Radical Christian Life* which begins on page 11 of this book invites your embrace of Benedictine values in a systematic way, set forth as pillars of Benedictine spirituality. If you are studying on your own, take each pillar as a day's meditation. If you are working with a group, you may want to address one of the pillars on pages 42-75 each week. Not every discussion question need be "answered." Choose the questions that intrigue you. One or two poems accompany each pillar, for those who meditate best with poetry, or those who might like to try it.

Approach your study and discussion of radical Christianity in the spirit that you are both active and contemplative. Expect your meditation on each of the six pillars of Benedictinism to bear real fruit, visible to the world. Expect it to lead you to do something. Consider, through my reflections and questions, in what ways the pillars run counter to the world as it is and point to the world as it could be. The imagination of something better is the first step on your path to it. The second step will not take place in your imagination, but in the world.

The Radical Christian Life:
An Exercise in Spiritual Imagination

By Joan Chittister

The Radical Christian Life:
An Exercise in Spiritual Imagination

There are two stories, one from the Sufi masters and one from the monastics of the desert, that may have a great deal to tell us about what it means to live a radical Christian life in our own times.

In the first, the Sufi tell about a spiritual elder who asked the disciples to name what was the most important quality in life: wisdom or action? "It's action, of course," the disciples said. "After all, of what use is wisdom that does not show itself in action?" "Ah, yes," the master said, "but of what use is action that proceeds from an unenlightened heart?" Or to put it another way, busyness alone is not enough to qualify us as a spiritual people. We must be busy about the right things.

In the second story from the desert monastics, Abba Poemen says of Abba John that John had prayed to God to take his passions away so that he might become free from care. "And, in fact," Abba John reported to him, "I now find myself in total peace, without an enemy." But Abba Poemen said to him, "Really? Well, in that case, go and beg God to stir up warfare within you again for it is by warfare that the soul makes progress." And after that when warfare came Abba John no longer prayed that it might be taken away. Now he simply prayed: "Lord, give me the strength for the fight."

Point: We are not meant to be long-distance observers of life. We are to give ourselves to the shaping of it, however difficult that may be in this day and age.

This commitment to co-creation is a great task, a noble task for which to give a life, but it is not a simple one. We are at a crossover moment in time—somewhere between the certainty of the past, the demands of the present, and the possibility of the future. It is a moment again in human history that needs deep wisdom and requires holy struggle.

At the dawn of the twenty-first century, the world is shifting. In fact, the world is dizzyingly mobile now. As a culture, we are shifting away from being isolationist and independent to being global and interdependent.

It is a world where "Catholic and Protestant" have melted into simply being Christians together and our new neighbors and their temples, monasteries, and mosques are Hindu, Buddhist, Jewish, and Muslim.

Our task now is to be radical Christian communities—in the here and now—not fossils of a bygone reality, not leftovers from an earlier golden age. Now we need new wisdom and a new kind of struggle to determine what we must be and do in the midst of these changing times.

Our choices are clear: We can go forward again and become something new in order to leaven the new or we can go backward in an attempt to maintain what we know better but which is already gone.

The question is then: What does it mean to be a radical Christian community in times such as these? And how do we do it?

The choice is ours. But, don't be fooled: not only is it not an easy choice; it is not an easy task.

The very map of the world is changing as we stand here: People are starving to death on the television screens in our family rooms. People who have worked hard all their lives fear for their retirement while we continue to put more money into instruments of destruction in this society than we do into programs for human development. The economy is in a state of skew. Only those who do not have to work are really making money. And, at the same time, there are a growing number of very rich and an even greater number of very, very poor.

Life is counted as nothing. Abortion is the most popular form of birth control in developing countries.

Hundreds, thousands, of civilians everywhere—most of them women and children—die in wars that men design to "protect them." And we continue to practice capital punishment even though we know that this so-called "deterrence," which makes us just like what we hate, does not deter. In fact, the ten states without capital punishment have lower murder rates than those that do.

Christians, serious seekers, now must choose either to retire from this fray into some paradise of marshmallow pieties where they can massage away the questions of the time, the injustice of the age, with spiritual nosegays and protests of powerlessness— where they can live like pious moles in the heart of a twisted world and call that travesty peace and "religion"—or they can gather their strength for the struggle it will take to bring this world closer to the reign of God now.

But what can possibly be done in this runaway world of the powerful few by the rest of us who hold no malice and want no wars, who have no influence but hold high ideals, who call ourselves Christian and claim to mean it!

Who are we now? And who do we want to be?

Most of all, where can we possibly go for a model of how to begin to be a radical Christian witness in a society in which we are almost totally remote from its centers of power and totally outside its centers of influence?

My suggestion is that we stop drawing our sense of human effectiveness from the periods of exploration and their destruction of native peoples, or from the period of industrialization and its displacement of people, or from the periods of the world wars and their extermination of peoples.

My suggestion is that little people—people like you and me—begin to look again to the sixth century and to the spiritual imagination and wondrous wisdom that made it new. Because that is really the good news.

An Ancient Model

In the sixth century, Benedict of Nursia was an aspiring young student at the center of the empire with all the glitz and glamour, all the fading glory and dimming power, that implied.

Rome had overspent, overreached, and overlooked the immigrants on the border who were waiting—just waiting—to pour through the system like a sieve.

Rome—ROME!—the invincible, had been sacked. As in the book of Daniel, the handwriting was on the wall, but few, if anyone, read it.

In our own world, the headlines are in our papers, too, and few, if any, are reading them.

But in the sixth century, one person, this young man, resolved to change the system not by confronting it, not by competing with it to be bigger, better, or more successful but by eroding its incredible credibility.

As Blaise Pascal would write: "It is true that force rules the world but opinion looses force."

This one single person in the sixth century—without the money, the technology, the kind of systemic support our age considers so essential to success and therefore uses to explain its failure to make a difference—simply refused to become what such a system modeled and came to have a major influence in our own time.

This one person simply decided to change people's opinions about what life had to be by himself living otherwise, by refusing to accept the moral standards around him, by forming other people into organized communities to do the same: to outlaw slavery where they were; to devote themselves to the sharing of goods as he was; to commit themselves to care for the earth; to teach and model a new perspective on our place in the universe.

The Radical Christian Life

And on his account—though numbers, history attests, were never his criteria for success—thousands more did the same age after age after age.

For over 1,500 years, popes and peoples across the centuries have called Benedict of Nursia the patron of Europe and accredited the Benedictine lifestyle that he developed in the darkest periods of Western history with the very preservation of European culture.

The values it modeled maintained the social order. And safeguarded learning. And gave refuge to travelers. And made rules for war that brought peace to chaos.

Those values turned a Europe devastated by invasion and neglect into a garden again. They modeled the equality of peoples. They provided a link between heaven and earth—between this life, chaotic as it was, and the will of God for all of life. Everywhere. Always.

But how was all of that done? And what does it have to do with us today? The answer upends everything our own society insists is essential to effectiveness.

The very model of life that Benedict of Nursia gave the world was exactly the opposite of what, in the end, was really destroying it.

To a world that valued bigness—big villas, big cities, big armies, big systems—Benedict gave a series of small and intense communities where people of one mind gathered to support one another, to find the strength for the fight. Their struggle was for survival, but their strength was community.

To an empire with a global reach—France, Britain, Egypt, Constantinople—Benedict gave an unending line of local groups whose solicitude for the people and understanding of the issues of the area from which they came was built into their very DNA. The struggle of such small groups was for survival, yes; but their strength was total engagement in the human condition.

To an empire intent on the centralization of all cultures into one, Benedict gave a model of autonomy, of agency, of individual self-development to a culture that accepted both submission and slavery far, far too easily. The struggle against such odds was for survival, yes; but their strength was a sense of human dignity and personal possibility—in an era that had neither.

To a world with a bent for monuments meant to mark the history and the glory of an empire, Benedict abandoned the notion of a joint institutional history and built a common tradition out of many separate parts instead. The struggle was for survival of these autonomous small groups. Their strength was the singular commitment bred in each separate group to each carry the fullness of the tradition.

In a civic order strictly defined by specific roles and responsibilities, Benedict chose instead to create a lifestyle rather than to define a fixed work that the years could erode or the culture could abandon. The struggle was surely for survival; but the surety of that in every group was creativity and adaptation.

In a world made up of powerful institutions Benedict did not create an institution; instead, he started a movement—a loose collection of similarly serious and equal seekers who gave the world new ways of thinking about autocracy and narcissism, oppression and injustice, inequality and authoritarianism. The struggle was indeed survival; the strength was an energy and dynamism that affected the whole society.

And finally, in a world where the word of an emperor meant death, Benedict built a world where the word of God gave new life day after day after day to everyone it touched.

A Tradition that Transforms

And little by little, this little movement of serious seekers, small rather than large, local rather than global, autonomous rather than centralized, more intent on a common tradition than a common history, more a movement than an institution, more committed to the Gospel than to the system—bound together as equal adults in communities of heart and mind they crept up slowly on the culture around them, they seduced its hardness of heart, they converted its soul, and, in one small place after another, they made the world whole again.

So why does it work? What can something so small, so fragile, possibly be able to give to a world like that?

How is it that something built on individual members in small individual houses for which survival is always the order of the day can possibly have "saved European culture" and then spread across the whole wide world? After all, individual Benedictine monasteries have come and gone in great number century after century but the tradition has lived on.

The fact is that Benedict left us a very simple structure, yes, but he left it standing on very deep pillars.

He established it on values that spanned the whole human experience—not on rules or specific works that would crash and crumble with the crumbling of the time and cultures.

He based the life on human and spiritual insights that never go out of style: on foundational human needs, for instance, like community and work and service; on profound spiritual practices, like prayer and contemplation and humility; on major social issues, like stewardship and hospitality, equality and peace; on basic organizational givens, like leadership and communal decision making, on mutual service and mutual obedience.

And so as every era grappled with its own agendas and issues, the importance or consciousness of each of these Benedictine values became the gift Benedictines gave to a culture out of sync with its own best interests.

In early Benedictinism, community itself and the need for hospitality, generated by the breakdown of public security that came with the fall of the empire, was the issue. When pilgrims and travelers were being raped, robbed, and pillaged on the roads, these communities built guesthouses—whole hospitality centers—to protect them.

In the Middle Ages, the need for agricultural development and social services became paramount. When whole tracts of land were burned out by war or fell into disuse, when crops died for want of good husbandry, when the peasants were starving and without work, small communities set up granges—small missions of three or four monastics—to organize the laborers and distribute the crops to the poor. And they did these things while they tried, at the same time, to make rules for war that would mitigate its effects and control the seemingly endless insanity that was destroying, ironically, exactly what was being fought for.

With the rise of cities and the dawn of commercialization, the creation of spiritual and educational centers became a major Benedictine concern. Where learning became a thing of the past and whole areas were left spiritually starved, monasteries took upon themselves the preservation of ancient texts and became the spiritual refuge of the poor, the homeless, the oppressed.

In the nineteenth century European Benedictine monasteries sent some of their best to the new world to do the same. It was a world of Catholic versus Protestant cultures, a dying but still potent remnant of the wars of religion long centuries past. The Benedictine task in the new world was to educate Catholic immigrant populations to take their place in a world that was largely WASP—white, Anglo-Saxon, and Protestant. It was a very radical Christian mission for that time to educate the poor and illiterate, integrate sharply divided worldviews into a democratic whole, and adjust to the kind of pluralism the world had never known. And it was successful.

Through it all, for centuries—centuries—Benedictine communities—small, local, and autonomous—worked in creative ways to meet the needs of the areas in which they grew, struggling always to shape and balance a deep and communal spiritual life with the great social needs around them.

They gifted every age out of the treasures of the heart that are the pillars of Benedictinism. As a result, they grew and they concentrated and they specialized and they changed till there were as many slightly different but all basically the same Benedictine monasteries as there were stripes on a zebra.

If the twenty-first century needs anything at all, it may well be a return to the life-giving, radical vision of Benedict. Perhaps we need a new reverence for bold Benedictine wisdom if civilization is to be saved again—and this time the very planet preserved.

The values that saved Western Europe in a social climate akin to our own were creative work, not profit making; holy leisure, not personal escapism; wise stewardship, not exploitation; loving community, not individualism raised to the pathological; humility, not arrogant superiority; and a commitment to peace, not domination. Today, just as 1,500 years ago, those values have been foresworn.

We dearly need them again.

The Pillars of
Benedictine Spirituality

Creative Work

This age needs to rethink work. Work in our time has either become something that defines us or something that oppresses us. We do it to make money, money, money or we decry it as an obstacle to life. We are a culture that too often stands between workaholism and pseudo-contemplation.

For years I watched Sophie, an old Polish lady across the street from the monastery, sweep the sidewalk in front of her house with a strong and steady hand and then move methodically to the front of the houses to her left and to her right.

She became, in fact, a kind of neighborhood joke, doing a fruitless task. After all, the street was spotless already, wasn't it? What was the use of this senseless monotony?

And then she died.

Newer, younger neighbors moved into her house who had no time, no interest, in sweeping sidewalks. And the street has never been clean since.

Sophie reminded me again what Benedict's commitment to work was meant to teach us. I recognized in her that the work we do is not nearly so determining as why we do it.

Work—every kind of work: manual, intellectual, spiritual—is meant to be the human being's contribution to the development of the human race.

The Benedictine works to complete the work of God in the upbuilding of the world. We work, as well, to complete ourselves. We become more skilled, more creative, more effective. When we work we discover that we really are "good for something."

Work, the Benedictine sees, is an asceticism that is not contrived, not symbolic. It's real. It is a task that puts me in solidarity with the poor for whom the rewards of labor are few and far between while the rigors are constant and security is tenuous.

Work is our gift to the future, and if the work we do is a contribution to the order and the coming of the reign of God, and if we do it well, like Sophie, it will be needed, and when we are not there to do it, it will be missed.

Holy Leisure

This age needs to rethink leisure, as well. Play and holy leisure are not the same things. Leisure is the Benedictine gift of regular reflection and continual consciousness of the presence of God. It is the gift of contemplation in a world of action.

Holy leisure is a necessary respite from a wildly moving world that turns incessantly now on technology that grants neither the space nor the time it takes to think.

I remember the day some years ago when a reporter called to ask for an interview on some document that had just been released from Rome.

"I can't talk to you about that," I said. "I haven't seen it and I don't comment on anything I haven't had a chance to read and study."

"Well," he said, "if I send it to you, will you talk to me about it then?"

I calculated the time: This was Thursday. The document couldn't possibly arrive in the mail before Monday, so I figured I could meet the deadline I was working on now and get the new document read before he called.

"All right," I said, "You can send it."

A few minutes later I heard a clacking sound coming from an office down the hall.

"What is that?" I said to the sister in the office.

"It's the fax machine," she said. "It's something for you from New York and it's already over eighty pages long. There's a note on it about calling you back to talk about it this afternoon."

This is a world high on technology, short on time, starved for reflection.

Benedictine leisure is a life lived with a continuing commitment to the development of a culture with a Sabbath mind.

The rabbis teach that the purpose of Sabbath is threefold: First, to make everyone—slave and citizen alike—free for at least one day a week.

Second, to give us time to do what God did: To evaluate our work to see if it is good.

And finally, the rabbis say, the purpose of Sabbath is to reflect on life, to determine whether what we're doing and who we are is what we should be doing and who we want to be. Sabbath is meant to bring wisdom and action together. It provides the space we need to begin again.

If anything has brought the modern world to the brink of destruction it must surely be the loss of holy leisure.

When people sleep in metro stations it is holy leisure that asks why.

When babies die for lack of medical care it is holy leisure that asks why.

When thousands of civilians die from "death by drones"—unmanned aerial predators that bomb their lands and lives unmercifully—it is holy leisure that asks, how that can possibly be of God.

To give people space to read and think and discuss the great issues of the time from the perspective of the Gospel may be one of Benedictinism's greatest gifts to a century in which the chaos of action is drying up humanity's deepest wells of wisdom.

Dom Cuthbert Butler wrote once: "It is not the presence of activity that destroys the contemplative life; it is absence of contemplation."

Holy leisure is the foundation of contemplation and contemplation is the ability to see the world as God sees the world. Indeed, the contemplative life will not be destroyed by activity but by the absence of contemplation.

In Benedictine spirituality, life is not divided into parts, one holy and the other mundane. To the Benedictine mind all of life is holy. All of life's actions bear the scrutiny of all of life's ideals. All of life is to be held with anointed hands.

Who shall lead them into a contemplative life if not we?

Stewardship

The spirituality of stewardship, one of Benedictinism's strongest, greatest gifts, must be rethought in our time.

The 401 pounds of garbage per U.S. citizen that the world cannot dispose of is made up of the Styrofoam cups we use and the tin cans we've discarded rather than recycled while the rest of the world reuses three to five times as much material as we do. Humans today are polluting earth, sea, and sky at a rate unheard of in any other period of history and we in the United States more than most.

But Benedictines before us brought order and organization, learning, Scripture and art, the tools of civilization and the sustenance of the soul.

They used every human form of education and skill to bring order out of chaos, equality to the masses, and healing to their world. Benedictines before us tilled dry land and made it green. They dried the swamps and made them grow. They seeded Europe with crops that fed entire populations, they raised the cattle that gave new life, they distilled liquors and brewed hops that brought joy to the heart and health to the body. It is not possible to live life with a Benedictine heart and fail to nurture the seeds of life for every living creature.

How, as Benedictines, if we are serious seekers, can we possibly build now what is not green? How can we soak our lands in chemicals and grow what is not organic? How can we possibly, as Benedictines, use what is not disposable and never even call a community meeting on the consequences to others of our doing so?

To allow ourselves to become chips in an electronic world, isolates in a cemented universe, women and men out of touch with the life pulse of a living God, indifferent to creation, concerned only with ourselves, and still call ourselves good is to mistake the rituals of religion for the sanctifying dimensions of spirituality.

The serious seeker knows that we are here to become the voices for life in everything everywhere—as have done our ancestors before us for over 1,500 years.

Benedictine spirituality, the spirituality that brought the world back from the edge before, asks us to spend our time well, to contemplate the divine in the human, to treat everything in the world as sacred. We need the wisdom of stewardship now.

Community

Community is a concept that our age must reexamine and renew. An old woman in my Pennsylvania hometown lived alone in her own home till the day she died. The problem is that she died eighteen months before her body was found because no one ever came to visit her, no one called to see if she had gotten her prescriptions, no one checked when her water was turned off for lack of payment. And there are thousands like her in this world of ours.

And how are we reaching out to them? Benedictine community assumes by its very nature that we exist to be miracle workers to one another. It is in human community that we are called to grow. It is in human community that we come to see God in the other. It is in its commitment to build community that Benedictinism must be a sign to a world on the verge of isolation.

But a Benedictine spirituality of community calls for more than togetherness—the very cheapest sort of community. Communal spirituality calls for an open mind and an open heart. It centers us on the Jesus who was an assault on every closed mind in Israel.

To those who thought that illness was punishment for sin, Jesus called for openness. To those who considered tax collectors incapable of salvation, Jesus called for openness. To those who believed that the Messiah—to be real—had to be a military figure, Jesus was a call to openness.

The Benedictine heart—the heart that saved Europe—is a place without boundaries, a place where the truth of the oneness of the human community shatters all barriers, opens all doors, refuses all prejudices, welcomes all strangers, and listens to all voices.

Community cannot be taken for granted. We must ask ourselves always who it is who is uncared for and unknown—dying from loneliness, prejudice, or pain—and waiting for your community and mine to knock on the door, to seek them out, to take them in, to hold them up till they can live again.

Real community requires mindfulness of the whole human condition—so that the spirit that is Benedictine may spread like a holy plague throughout the world.

Humility

Humility needs to be rediscovered if we are to take our rightful place in the world in this age. It was July 20, 1969, the night the United States landed the first man on the moon. I was standing next to a foreign exchange teacher who had come from Mexico to teach Spanish for us.

"Well," I laughed, looking up into the dark night sky, "There's the man in our moon." I could almost hear her bristle beside me. In a tight, terse voice she said back, "It is not your moon!"

At that moment I got a lesson in Benedictine humility, in international relations and racism and multiculturalism that springs from it, that no novice mistress had been able to articulate nearly as well.

Humility is about learning your place in the universe, about not making either yourselves or your nation anybody's god. It is about realizing that we are all equal players in a common project called life.

Learning like that can change your politics. It will certainly change your humanity—your soul.

In a culture that hoards money and titles and power and prestige like gold, Benedict makes the keystone value of his rule of life a chapter on humility that was written for Roman men in a society that valued machoism, power, and independence at least as much as ours.

It is the antidote to an achievement-driven, image-ridden, competitive society that is the hallmark of the modern age.

Humility, the acceptance of our earthiness, is also the antidote to the myth of perfectionism that, masking as holiness, can sink the soul in despair and lead it to abandon the very thought of a truly spiritual life in the face of the very failures we fear.

It makes us look again at our so-called patriotism, our sexism, our racisms, and our narcissism, both personal and national.

It makes us look again even at our spiritual arrogance in the face of the world's other great spiritual traditions.

Most of all, it enables us to learn and to grow and never to be disappointed in what we don't get in life because, we come to realize, it isn't ours to claim in the first place.

We need the wisdom of humility now. We need that quality of life that makes it possible for people to see beyond themselves, to value the other, to touch the world gently, peacefully, and make it better as we go.

Peace

We must, most of all, in our time, rethink the meaning of peace. Over the archway of every medieval monastery were carved the words, *Pax intrantibus*, "Peace to those who enter here."

The words were both a hope and a promise. In a culture struggling with social chaos, Benedict sketched out a blueprint for world peace. He laid a foundation for a new way of life, the ripples of which stretched far beyond the first monastery arch to every culture and continent from one generation to another, from that era to this one, from his time and now to ours. To us.

That is our legacy, our mandate, our mission—as alive today as ever, more in need in today's nuclear world than ever before.

Once we could teach that the United States' major export was wheat. Now we have to admit that weapons are. We arm 250 different countries every year and provide almost half of all the arms sold in the world while we decry the selling of them.

Indeed, as Benedictines we must rethink our own commitment to Benedictine peace and our obligation to proclaim it in this world. Benedictine peace, however, is not simply a commitment to the absence of war. It is, as well, the presence of a lifestyle that makes war unacceptable and violence unnecessary.

Even if we dismantled all the war machines of the world tomorrow, it would be no guarantee that we would have peace. The armies of the world simply demonstrate the war that is going on in our souls, the restlessness of the enemy within us, the agitation of the human condition gone awry.

To all these things we need to bring a new spiritual imagination. Imagine a world where people choose their work according to the good it will do for the poorest of the poor—because they saw it in us.

Imagine a world where holy leisure, spiritual reflection rather than political expedience, began to determine everything we do as a nation—because they saw it in us.

Imagine a world where the care of the earth became a living, breathing, determining goal in every family, every company, every life we touch—because they saw it in us.

Imagine a world devoted to becoming a community of strangers that crosses every age level, every race, every tradition, every difference on the globe—because they saw it in us.

Imagine a world where humble listening to the other became more important than controlling them— because people saw it in us.

Imagine a world where what makes for peace becomes the foundation of every personal, corporate, and national decision—because they were called to it by us.

And now imagine what communities inspired by Benedict can do, should do, will do—consciously, corporately, conscientiously—to bring these things into being in every area, region, street, city, institution here and now.

Let us resolve again to follow the fiery-eyed radical Benedict of Nursia whose one life illuminated Western civilization. Let us, in other words, live Benedictine spirituality and illuminate our own darkening but beautiful world.

On the Dialogues of Gregory

A follower of Benedict who became Pope Gregory the Great is attributed with preserving the life of Saint Benedict in a document called The Dialogues of Gregory. The Dialogues are the only source of biographical materials that we have on either Benedict or his sister, Scholastica. Through stories in the metaphorical style of the time, the Dialogues give insight into their personal qualities and character of soul rather than a recitation of simple historical details. The stories are fanciful to modern ears, perhaps, but logical to the heart. These are the things of which real humanity is made: the spiritual life and the human community. As a result, Benedict and

Scholastica do not shine in the human constellation of stars because of who or what they are as individuals. No, Benedict and Scholastica stand out in history because of what their lives did for the centuries of lives that would follow them.

It is my belief that the way of life established by Benedict over 1,500 years ago is a gift to our times, a beacon in the dark showing us still how to live well.

Deep Wisdom, Holy Struggle

Exploring the Radical Christian Life

By Barbara Cawthorne Crafton

Deep Wisdom, Holy Struggle

Creative Work

I pride myself on being a hard worker. Exactly whose approval I seek with my long hours and many tasks, I long ago gave up asking myself—a packed agenda is too integral a part of who I am for that. I do enjoy the productivity of being this way, and I do think my work matters, but I also know its hazards: at my most driven, I resemble nothing so much as a hamster on a wheel.

Of course my work matters—I work for the church! Everything I *do* is important. But each project is dispensed only to go on immediately to the next one, with little time in between to reflect on either of them. Often I have been divided within myself about my work: convinced of its importance, satisfied with my performance of it but curiously flat about each task's contribution to the overall sufficiency of my ministry. I flatter myself that I conceal this well, but I am probably mistaken about that. People aren't stupid.

Church work though this may be, and as important as it may be, it has far to go before it could be considered holy work. There is a world of spiritual difference between holy work and having a job. So, though parish ministry calls for as much creativity as I can muster, it is to writing that I turn to experience my work as anything akin to what the Benedictines mean by the term "creative work."

But if this is so, why do I allow my parish work to suck precious moments from what little time I have for writing, when no emergency forces me to do so? Why do I go for days without writing, when I love to write? And what am I to make of the strange fits of sloth that overtake me when I sit down at the computer, causing me to play game after game of computer solitaire instead of turning to the blank page that tugs at my sleeve? I sabotage my creative work with silly distractions, endangering both my work and my deadline.

I call my psychologist friend. *Why don't you think of the person for whom you're writing this*, he says. *If you can't seem to do it for you, maybe you can do it for her.* I hear him out, and think maybe we're getting somewhere at last: the editor for this project is someone I like, and the team working on it are all people I respect. My contribution is important for the project's success. I can bear in mind the community for whose sake I work, as I struggle to stay on task.

The Jewish concept of work, codified in order to support the commandment to keep the Sabbath holy, famously stipulates all sorts of things to be work: carrying a handkerchief, walking more than 2000 cubits (about half a mile), turning a stove on or off, answering the telephone. Clearly, what is at stake in such painstaking definition is not only the energy expended or the product of work—these limits are not imposed solely out of concern about the activity itself.

It is where an activity might lead that presents a risk to Sabbath observance, and for the best of reasons: we human beings tend to increase our productivity once we get started. We think of new things to do. We embroider on our tasks, and in that embroidery lies the holiness of work: when work is holy to us—and "holy" may or may not have anything to do with what we ordinarily call "religious"—we take joy in doing it better than we need to.

The Benedictine works to complete the work of God in the upbuilding of the world, says Joan Chittister. We work, as well, to complete ourselves. So integral a part of being human is work, considered in this way, that philosophers have coined this descriptor for us: among the many things we are, we are *homo faber*, the human who makes things.

Holy work arises from our very nature. Far from being the curse imagined in Genesis 3:19, "In the sweat of thy face shalt thou eat bread" (King James Version Bible), work ennobles us by allowing us to experience something of what God knows in creating the universe and in creating us. Work is not a punishment—Adam, we are told, was placed in the Garden of Eden to work the land and take care of it before any of that dreadful business with the serpent and the forbidden fruit took place. Work has always been part of who we are.

I have said that work need not be explicitly religious to be holy. Similarly, the measure of work's creativity is not derived from its status in the eyes of the world. Viewed through the prism of holiness, these is no such thing as a menial task. This is not to say that every swipe of a soapy sponge across your kitchen counter should be laden with overwrought symbolic imaginings, only that the cleaning of your home—just the orderly fact of doing it—matters, even if no one applauds or even sees.

The homeliest of tasks is ennobled if it is done in the service of the community, however large or small the community may be. Most of the work in caring for an infant, for example—the feeding, the wiping of noses and bottoms and tears, the changing of diapers—would be considered unpleasant if it were performed for anybody else, but it all feels like love to a loving parent, most of the time.

And yet, there is a reason we don't call it "play." Holy work may be holy, but it is still effortful. It might at times be painful. It can be tedious. Work carries with it the possibility of failure; sometimes our most earnest efforts do not succeed. It is true that Adam and Eve worked before their famous fall from grace, but the curse pronounced upon human work afterwards was left to us by the ancient storytellers because it conveys an additional truth about work: not all of it *is* holy. We can become estranged from the fruits of our labor. Chattel slavery can deny them to us, giving to another profit we have earned. So can less obvious forms of slavery: the estrangement of the worker from the fruits of his labor— and, in modern times, even from the completion of its product—can suck work dry of meaning.

We don't make things, many of us. We make parts of things, unrecognizable as components of any future whole. And much of our work could not accurately be characterized as "making" anything at all: some of us cause money to fly around the world electronically, sending letters and reports about it out through the internet, receiving our payment for doing so by the same means. My treasurer hopes I will not wish to receive a paper check he must write out and sign; he hopes I will elect to receive my salary by direct deposit into my bank. And I oblige. The check is no longer in the mail; it is in the ether.

The community work creates has changed, too. I worked with my webmaster for two years before we ever met face to face. I have never met the editor of my last book. Do you know so-and-so, someone asks, and I pause. How to answer? I've worked feverishly with so-and-so by email to complete a complicated project, but we would not recognize each other were we to meet on the street, which we probably never will.

So, do I know her, or do I not?

Creative work builds the community in which it is performed, and the worker himself is part of that community. There must be a sturdy link between them, a strong sense of working for the community's sake. The idea that everyone pursuing her own interest will vector automatically into the public good is the opposite of what creative work aims to produce: the communal spirit in which work is performed is as central to its character as its product.

For Discussion

1.   Sketch a timeline of your employment history. What does it reveal? Have you always done the same type of work, or has your career been more varied? Which of the jobs you have held do you think of as holy work? Remember that holy work need not be religious in nature; it is work that builds both the world and you.

2.   Sketch a timeline of your history of unpaid work, including the work of maintaining your home and caring for your family. Which of your avocations do you regard as creative work? How did they become part of your life?

3.   What is the community for whose sake you do your creative work? What is your attitude toward that community? Do you feel like a member of it?

4.   If your spirit responds better to art than to discourse, read this poem by a priest about a blacksmith in his

parish who has died, bearing in mind what we have said about creative work.

Felix Randal

Felix Randal the farrier,
*   O is he dead then? my duty all ended,*
Who have watched his mould of man,
*   big-boned and hardy-handsome*
Pining, pining, till time when reason rambled in it,
*   and some*
Fatal four disorders, fleshed there, all contended?

Sickness broke him. Impatient, he cursed at first,
*   but mended*
Being anointed and all; though a heavenlier heart
*   began some*
Months earlier, since I had our sweet reprieve and ransom
Tendered to him.
*   Ah well, God rest him all road ever he offended!*

This seeing the sick endears them to us, us too it endears.
My tongue had taught thee comfort,
*   touch had quenched thy tears,*
Thy tears that touched my heart, child,
*   Felix, poor Felix Randal;*

How far from then forethought of,
*   all thy more boisterous years,*

When thou at the random grim forge,
powerful amidst peers,
Didst fettle for the great grey drayhorse
his bright and battering sandal!

—Gerard Manley Hopkins, 1880

Holy Leisure

Not all leisure is holy leisure. Some of it is just goofing off—and there is a good case to be made for completely unproductive activity undertaken for no other reason than because it's fun. But we are not built for a steady diet of it; we enjoy our pure fun more when it is relatively rare.

The kind of leisure we consider here isn't goofing off. It is the intentional quiet space in which life-changing dreams can surface. There is a holy shape to this quiet time—it isn't just another round of golf or another trip to the shopping mall.

For this reason, your holy leisure may be assisted by being tied to a specific place or action—a chapel, a certain chair, a particular walk outdoors, an activity like knitting or fishing or sewing. Do the same thing in the same way in the same place often enough, and the thing itself, the place itself, will draw you into the mindfulness you seek. Taking yourself to your physical place for contemplation will accustom you to contemplating. It will trigger the emergence of your more mindful self.

Abiding in the place where your holy leisure has taken shape, you have space to ask yourself important questions. Who am I, and who are we? Is it really true that war is inevitable, that nothing can be done about world hunger? What if things were not as they are?

A mistaken dichotomy haunts our longing for holy leisure. Many people believe that there are spiritual people and there are social activists, and that they are not the same kind of people. This is not so. Everyone has a spiritual life, and everyone has a call to be a citizen of the world. The refreshment of holy leisure directly fuels the impulse to seek justice if we desire to have it so. Joan Chittister is as well known for her writing on the practice of prayer as for that on the moral issues of our time. Holy leisure permits prayer to deepen action, to judge rightly whether my outside matches my inside.

Holy leisure allows me to ask myself whether or not my action in society comports well with the person I know myself to be. The rock-bottom *me* I come to know in prayer is the *me* that God knows, rather than the half-dozen *me's* the world invites me to become in response to its welter of priorities.

For Discussion

1.   Make a list of the things you do for fun. Be inclusive—list anything you do that you enjoy, not just the ones that are "good for you." Include your endless rounds of "Angry Birds," as well as the hours you spend reading good books.

2.   Some of what you listed distracts you from thinking, and some provides space for it. Look at your list: Which is which? Is there a preponderance of one or the other?

3.   Draw a circle, representing a typical day in your life. Delineate the slice of the pie representing the time you spend sleeping. Then delineate another slice, the time you spend in creative work. This slice may or may not include your job—if it does not, make another slice for that, including your commute. Make a slice for the time you spend taking care of personal business—banking, visits to the doctor, etc. Make a slice for the time you spend goofing off. How much of your day remains for holy leisure?

4.   Remember a time when you allowed your mind to roam freely, and came up with something important: a change in your own life direction, a discovery of passion about a social or moral concern, a major shift of opinion about something important. What were you doing when this moment occurred?

5.   Do you recall a time when you were unable to do your ordinary activities? For example, a time when you were unable to work because of an injury or unemployment? Apart from the negative impact of such a reversal of fortune, did you gain anything from the increased time at your disposal? How did you use it? Looking back on it now, what can you say about that time?

6.   If you are working with this book in a group, consider together the priorities of the communities of which you are a part: your families, the organizations to which you belong, your towns, your nation. Where do these communities build space for the leisure that enables radical questions into their common life? Is there an

instrument for stopping and thinking? And, if there is none, where might it be created?

7.   Have you ever been on a corporate retreat? Not a silent one in a convent, but one in which the people in your workplace went off-site overnight? What was it like? What was its goal? Did it succeed?

8.   Thomas Gray took a walk through an old churchyard one day, and this poem was its result. Yes, it's a long one—and this is only a portion of it!—so don't struggle with every line in detail. Just read the excerpt beginning on page 56 aloud and let it come to you. It shows us the moral fruit of Gray's holy leisure. You can find a link to the full poem on the resources page at the end of this book.

Elegy Written In A Country Churchyard (excerpts)

The curfew tolls the knell of parting day,
The lowing herd wind slowly o'er the lea,
The ploughman homeward plods his weary way,
And leaves the world to darkness and to me. …

Beneath those rugged elms, that yew-tree's shade,
Where heaves the turf in many a mouldering heap,
Each in his narrow cell for ever laid,
The rude Forefathers of the hamlet sleep. …

Let not Ambition mock their useful toil,
Their homely joys, and destiny obscure;
Nor Grandeur hear with a disdainful smile
The short and simple annals of the poor. …

Nor you, ye Proud, impute to These the fault
If Memory o'er their Tomb no Trophies raise,
Where through the long-drawn aisle and fretted vault
The pealing anthem swells the note of praise. …

Perhaps in this neglected spot is laid
Some heart once pregnant with celestial fire;
Hands, that the rod of empire might have sway'd,
Or waked to ecstasy the living lyre.

But Knowledge to their eyes her ample page,
Rich with the spoils of time, did ne'er unroll;
Chill Penury repress'd their noble rage,
And froze the genial current of the soul.

Full many a gem of purest ray serene
The dark unfathom'd caves of ocean bear:
Full many a flower is born to blush unseen,
And waste its sweetness on the desert air. …

—THOMAS GRAY, 1750

Stewardship
and Community

The pillars of Benedictine spirituality flow from one another. Holy leisure gives rise to the discernment of creative work, and is, itself, experienced most profoundly as gift in light of the work which forms its backdrop. Creative work exists within the matrix of the community, and is performed for its sake.

The individual has no meaningful spiritual existence apart from the community of humankind, and lives in the creative tension of reinterpreting that citizenship in an ever-widening circle of inclusion. Therefore, separating stewardship and community in discussing *The Radical Christian Life* seems impossible to me.

The industriousness for which the vowed Benedictine life is famous, which made the monastic house a self-sufficient refuge from encroaching chaos and deprivation in medieval times, did not exist for the sake of its residents alone. The monasteries were also famous for their hospitality to the stranger. They combined these two virtues to offer education, farming and building technology, medical care, scholarship, and various kinds of refuge to the larger communities that surrounded them.

The Radical Christian Life is written against the backdrop of a contemporary society in which the idea of stewardship of the world's resources is under constant attack. Politically, it is almost impossible to secure a fiscal measure that demands a look further into the future than the end of the current quarter. Repeated economic disasters overtake the financial structures of nation after nation, rooted in a willingness to mortgage someone else's long-term future to one's own short-term gain.

This willingness has created the spurious conflict between environmental responsibility and economic growth, as if endlessly ignoring the environmental consequences of business decisions really were a viable way to proceed. In the name of individual liberty, courses of action which border on suicidal are defended with near-hysterical energy, often buttressed with the invocation of religion or patriotism. Witness the devoted defenses of fossil fuel use; of subsidized farming based on monoculture or the growing of a single crop on a farm or in a region; the insistence that any regulation of the financial industry constitutes restraint of trade, even in the light of hard evidence as to the consistent inability of these entities to regulate themselves.

This dismal state of affairs is what happens when the virtue of self-sufficiency is extended into absurdity. It becomes monstrous. Ownership replaces stewardship, and property rights trump human rights until people themselves become commodities. Nor is this the first time this has happened. Benedict's desire that his communities be able to sustain themselves became, as the societies in which they existed tumbled into chaos, as important to their neighbors as it was to the communities themselves. The monasteries' communal life was an example of what might be to people who would never live in vowed community.

Joan Chittister takes the silent tragedy of an elderly woman dying alone in her home as an example of the failure of community, and the multiple crises brought about by climate change as an example of the need for a new relationship to the world's resources. The ancient idea of "the common," an approach to community resources as old as America itself, one that came to these shores with the pilgrims and met with an even more communitarian spirit among the indigenous people they encountered, has disappeared. The posture dominant among us, that of ownership, necessarily defines community narrowly: *My significant community is me and my immediate family. I will take care of my own and you take care of your own, and all we need to agree on is to leave each other alone.*

One wonders: can a posture of stewardship versus one of ownership stand in an age when rapaciousness and greed have put on the mantle of holiness? When there's such a thing as a "Prosperity Church"? When the refusal to honor the insights of science into the workings of the natural world is used to bless the continued rape of the earth? When the possibility that human life might become unlivable because of human actions no longer seems remote?

What if I alone consider myself a steward, and everyone else considers himself an owner? Won't I just be trampled underfoot?

Well, perhaps. But at least I will know it is possible that my failure may still be a building block for a later generation's victory over violence and greed. The world in which Jesus of Nazareth lived certainly accounted him a failure! The prophetic road is not the easy road. Here, perhaps more than in any other aspect of Benedictinism as described in the introduction to *The Radical Christian Life*, the twin values of community and stewardship demand a prophetic stance—not just lived within the walls, but proclaimed without.

For Discussion

1.   Many scientists say now that it is too late to prevent the climate change global warming will cause, and that our task now is to deal with its effects. Given the dominance of ownership over stewardship in Western culture, where do you see evidence of our capacity to do this in some way other than "every man for himself"? How would society have to change in order to enable us to survive and maintain human community? Given the absence of the political will to mandate restraint in the management of our common resources, what might make so vast a change possible?

2.   The twentieth-century writer Ayn Rand wrote, "Civilization is the progress toward a society of privacy. The savage's whole existence is public, ruled by the laws of his tribe. Civilization is the process of setting man free from men" (*The Fountainhead*, 1943). From this perspective, personal freedom becomes the only moral imperative: there is really no such thing as society, only aggregations of individuals, each seeking his or her own good. Under such an assumption, would there be

any need for community? What about the ownership/ stewardship dichotomy? What would community be like if we acknowledged no duty to anyone but ourselves?

3. Have someone in the group make a case for the posture described in question two above in a "debate" as you discuss community and stewardship. How do you think this posture works with Christian faith, for those Christians who articulate it? Your "debate" is liable to lead the group quickly into a political discussion, and some may object, to say that they are uncomfortable when a spiritual discussion "gets political." Why do you think people say this? What makes us so uncomfortable with it? Do you think such a disturbance of our comfort is necessary to our becoming active in the pursuit of genuine community?

4. What might the poem on the next page be saying to us about stewardship and community?

Richard Cory

Whenever Richard Cory went down town,
We people on the pavement looked at him:
He was a gentleman from sole to crown,
Clean favored, and imperially slim.

And he was always quietly arrayed,
And he was always human when he talked;
But still he fluttered pulses when he said,
'Good-morning,' and he glittered when he walked.

And he was rich—yes, richer than a king—
And admirably schooled in every grace:
In fine, we thought that he was everything
To make us wish that we were in his place.

So on we worked, and waited for the light,
And went without the meat, and cursed the bread;
And Richard Cory, one calm summer night,
Went home and put a bullet through his head.

—Edwin Arlington Robinson, 1897

Humility

Humility is about learning your place in the universe, says Joan Chittister. We have turned to Adam and Eve before in this study guide, when we were considering creative work. We can look to them now as figures of the failure of humility. This was original sin: they refused to acknowledge a power and a freedom greater than their own.

But humility is more complex and more demanding than mere self-abnegation. It is as wrongheaded to refuse to acknowledge one's own gifts and powers as it is to claim gifts and powers one does not possess. To deny my capabilities is also to refuse to use them, for my own good or for that of anyone else. In a real sense, "humility" and "realism" are synonyms—humility is neither self-aggrandizing nor falsely modest. Thus, humility is organically related to stewardship: the stewardship of the talents God really has given me. In this, as in all things, the perfect is the enemy of the good: it is a neurotic version of humility that cannot own success or even dare aspire to it.

Humility is also much more than just an individual virtue. Joan Chittister approaches humility from the viewpoint of cultural and national notions of superiority. The curious incident she relates, in which her innocent remark about the first moon landing evokes a resentful response from a foreign visitor, both deepens and broadens our understanding of humility, carrying it far beyond the pious denial of self we usually think of in connection with it.

Original sin, it turns out, is every bit as corporate as it is individual. Even more, perhaps, because it snakes in among good impulses like love of one's family, love of one's faith, love of one's country and twists them into insularity, intolerance, and imperialism. The humility to which Joan Chittister calls us is corporate as well as individual, the bold abdication of a throne not rightfully ours.

For Discussion

1. Both the Hebrew and Christian scriptures assume God's special favor toward Israel (the chosen people) and then toward Christianity (the new Jerusalem). Talk together about how the notion of being chosen relates to the Benedictine virtue of humility. What does it mean to be chosen?

2. Talk together about evangelism and humility. What are the implications of John 14:6, "I am the way, and the truth, and the life. No one comes to the Father except through me," for the relationship of an evangelist to the one he or she seeks to convert?

3. How does a person in a position of authority exercise the virtue of humility? Have you ever known one who did? Have you ever known one who did not? What were these persons' roles? How did he or she show humility or lack of humility?

4. Much is made in recent political discourse of "American Exceptionalism." Most people who use the phrase today think of it as an unqualified good, but it was actually coined as a skeptical academic term to describe the assumption that God had a special plan for the United States. What might be the dangers of the current view of "American Exceptionalism"?

5. Here is a poem that may spark a discussion about corporate humility.

Ozymandias

I met a traveler from an antique land
Who said: Two vast and trunkless legs of stone
Stand in the desert. Near them, on the sand,
Half sunk, a shattered visage lies, whose frown,
And wrinkled lip, and sneer of cold command,
Tell that its sculptor well those passions read
Which yet survive, stamped on these lifeless things,
The hand that mocked them, and the heart that fed;
And on the pedestal these words appear:
"My name is Ozymandias, king of kings:
Look on my works, ye Mighty, and despair!"

Nothing beside remains. Round the decay
Of that colossal wreck, boundless and bare
The lone and level sands stretch far away.

— Percy Bysshe Shelly, 1818

Peace

Joan Chittister approaches peace from the inside out, beginning not with the banning of war's technological implements and the reasoned defeat of its political excuses, but with the transformation of the spirit, heart by heart. The reliance of the Benedictine movement upon attraction rather than coercion, its willingness to lead by example and its patience with the time it takes to lead in such a way convinces Chittister that peace, the crown of the Benedictine way, is a composition of all the other virtues we have discussed.

Because they saw it in us, she repeats again and again, as she dreams of a society at peace. A life balanced between creative work and holy leisure, lived in accountable community, holding its possessions lightly and in trust for those who come after with a realistic sense of limits and possibilities, will be a life of peace. A society ordered the same way will be a society at peace.

I have known people of peace. I have also known peaceful families, and peaceful monastic communities. Communal peace is anything but the magical thing those outside the community think it is. It requires consistent work and attention. It is hard won. But even the struggle for peace is hearteningly human. Communities that strive for peace can only do so through an intrepid genuineness, the rigorous honesty willing to name the beast within as well as the beast without.

I am not sure I know of a larger society at peace. It may be that size itself defeats the purposes of peace. Beyond a certain mass, the weight of institutional self-preservation crushes the accountability the other virtues need to rely on to grow among the members of that society. Joan Chittister identifies smallness as an aid to the pursuit of peace, and maybe it is so. Perhaps the peace of which we speak remains an ideal, drawing us along the road toward it but never within our grasp.

For Discussion

1. Do you a know a peaceful person? Make a list of his or her attributes, remembering the pillars of Benedictine spirituality as you do so. Can you name other peaceful people and their attributes? Do you find you know more peaceful people than you thought you did? What attributes do they have in common?

2. Is your community peaceful? Your church, perhaps, or another community important to you? List its attributes as you did the peaceful people you know. How does this community manage disagreement when it occurs? If the group with which you are studying radical Christianity is composed of people who are all members of the same community, such as a parish, consider this question as it applies to that community.

3. What about a larger community, such as a country? Can you think of a human community of which you have known, larger than a church, that has been at peace?

4. Here is a poem, another by the priest Gerard Manley Hopkins. Listen to its longing for peace at the beginning and the sternness of what peace requires at the end. Note the date of the poem—the terrible carnage of World War I is just ending.

Peace

When will you ever, Peace, wild wooddove, shy wings shut,
Your round me roaming end, and under be my boughs?
When, when, Peace, will you, Peace? I'll not play hypocrite
To own my heart: I yield you do come sometimes; but
That piecemeal peace is poor peace. What pure peace
allows
Alarms of wars, the daunting wars, the death of it?

O surely, reaving Peace, my Lord should leave in lieu
Some good! And so he does leave Patience exquisite,
That plumes to Peace thereafter.
And when Peace here does house
He comes with work to do, he does not come to coo,
He comes to brood and sit.

—Gerard Manley Hopkins, 1918

Where do we go from here?

It would be a shame if a book intended to seed transformative action arising from spiritual conversation left those who considered it exactly as they were before. I am sure you have identified more than one area in which your vision of the world in its current state is disturbing. Much is not as it should be. The Benedictine response to this undeniable truth is never despair: it is always action.

The Benedictine way is nothing if not pragmatic. I am sure—especially if your study of the book has been conducted in a group—that possibilities for action have already arisen in the service of one or more of the Benedictine pillars.

From the serious essays of the introduction's consideration of the six pillars we skim the dozens of little stories in the meditations of *The Radical Christian Life*—some funny, some archaic, some wildly improbable. They are glimpses of countercultural bravery, intended to encourage us to believe that we, too, are brave enough to put our money—and our energy and our voices and our shoulders, however weak or strong they may be—where our spirits are.

For Discussion

1. Over the past five weeks you have reflected on what Joan Chittister describes as the six pillars of Benedictine spirituality. Which ones particularly spoke to your own life, either the life you currently live or the life you aspire to? Are there aspects of the six pillars that you would like to incorporate into your own life more intentionally? How will you do that?

2. How can we Christians be leaven of hope and action in our world, rather than taking part in social despair? What is the role of the church?

3. Think of someone you know who shows counter-cultural bravery. First, consider letting them know that they matter to you. Second, think about how their life might be an inspiration to you.

4.   If you've been discussing this book in a group, what has been the greatest gift of this group experience? How do you wish to honor that? Are there things you would like to see this group do besides meet—begin a project or ministry, for example? If others are interested, what are some first steps to make that a reality?

Additional Resources

This book was created to coincide with the 2012 Trinity Institute National Theological Conference, *Radical Christian Life: Equipping Ourselves for Social Change.* More resources related to *Deep Wisdom, Holy Struggle,* including additional poems and other discussion material, are available at www.trinitywallstreet.org/institute.

For additional resources on spiritual practices and Christian living, please visit Forward Movement's website at www.forwardmovement.org.

About the Authors

Barbara Cawthorne Crafton is an Episcopal priest and author. She heads The Geranium Farm, an institute for the promotion of spiritual growth. She is currently interim rector of St. Luke's Episcopal Church in Metuchen, New Jersey, and has served a number of churches, including Trinity Wall Street in Lower Manhattan. A spiritual director, Crafton leads retreats and teaches throughout the United States and abroad. Her many books include *Jesus Wept: When Faith and Depression Meet* (Jossey-Bass, 2009); *Some Things You Just Have to Live With* (Morehouse Publications, 2003); and *Meditations on the Psalms* (Morehouse Publications, 2003).

Joan Chittister is a Benedictine sister and international author and lecturer who has been a leading voice for the essential connection between spirituality and social action for more than three decades. She is an inspiring speaker and profound teacher who practices what she preaches in ministries to the inner city, in prisons, and in speaking truth to power. Chittister's most recent books include: *The Radical*

Christian Life (Liturgical Press, 2011); *Songs of the Heart* (Twenty-Third Publications, 2011); *The Monastery of the Heart* (Blue Bridge, 2011); and *The Rule of Benedict: A Spirituality for the 21st Century* (Crossroad, 2010).